Crossed To Oblivion

Grace Lalrinpari Hauzel

Published by Gumby Publishers, 2023.

Published by Gumby Publishers,
36 Saint John's Place
Freeport 11520-4618
New York, USA

Airhub 1425, UBX 6 Poyle Trading Estate,
Colndale Road, Colnbrook
Slough SL30AA
Berkshire, United Kingdom

First Edition: March 2023
Editor : Ignatius Maximus John Azmoun

Table of Contents

About The Author

Grace Lalrinpari Hauzel is an enthusiastic budding writer who has been writing short stories and poetries since she was 6 years old. She manifested her views on life, emphasizing the enigmatic and arduous journey which are often thought provoking. Grace writes about nature, human emotions and divine love, using human love as an allegory. Grace is notorious for being a sleepyhead, most importantly a blithesome person. Her literary skills have gained recognition and have been awarded various awards.

Preface

"Fate Fell Short" is a phrase used to describe a situation where one's hopes or plans are dashed due to unforeseeable circumstances. It is a reminder that, despite our best efforts, we cannot control everything in life. One might experience this feeling after putting in hours of work on a project, only to have it fail at the last minute due to a technical glitch. Or perhaps you were excited about a job opportunity, but fate had other plans and someone else was chosen for the position. Whatever the situation may be, it is important to remember that failure is a part of life and that we can always learn from our mistakes. Instead of dwelling on the disappointment, it is best to take what we can from the experience and move forward, knowing that we have grown stronger and more resilient in the process.

Grace Lalrinpari Hauzel
17th February, 2023

About The Book

Crossed To Oblivion is a poetry book by Grace Lalrinpari Hauzel. The book is a collection of powerful poems that delve into the complex and often confusing nature of human emotions. The poems in this book are incredibly raw and emotional. Grace's writing style is both haunting and beautiful, drawing the reader in with powerful imagery and evocative language. Crossed To Oblivion is a must-read for anyone who loves poetry, especially those who are looking for a collection that explores the depths of the human experience.

Serendipity's Game

Life's full of twists and turns
Paths we take and lessons learned
Thinking we're in control
But fate has a funny way of taking a toll
Serendipity's game, it's a hell of a ride
Throws you curves, takes you on a wild surprise
But when it's all said and done
You realize, you wouldn't change a thing, not even one
Sometimes we fight against the flow
Thinking we know where to go
But the universe has a plan
And it won't let you off the hook, not at your command
We can't control the hand we're dealt
But we can choose how we feel
Though fate may twist and turn
We can always learn, we can always heal
Serendipity's game, a game we can't win
But we keep playing, again and again
Cause when it's all said and done
We realize, fate's already won.

Fell

You walked into my life like a summer breeze
I didn't know how hard I'll fall, gave me a disease
You had me wrapped up in your fingertips
I was blinded by your beauty and all I could do was stare
Fell for you like a leaf in autumn
In a landslide, you took my heart
Fell for you like the rain in April
Couldn't resist, right from the start
I tried to take it slow, but you had me swept away
All I think about is you, every single day
Can't believe I'm this much of a fool
Struggling to stay sane, I'm under your spell
I never thought I'd fall this hard
But here I am, drowning in your love
Can't shake the feeling, can't break the chains
I'm at the mercy of your embrace
Can't help but feel this way
You had me from the very first day
Fell for you, there's no other way
Can't deny it, I'm here to stay.

Short Days

Short days, long nights
Can't seem to get you out of my sight
You're like a flame, burning bright
In the darkness, you're my light
Short days, but they feel so long
Can't wait to have you in my arms
If this is right, then nothing's wrong
You make my short days feel so strong
Every time, you come around
My heart starts beating with a loud sound
Can't help but smile, can't help but frown
You've got me feeling up and down
All the times we spend apart
Makes me feel like we're worlds apart
But when you're here, all I want to do
Is hold you tight, and never let go of you
Short days, but they feel so long
Can't wait to have you in my arms
If this is right, then nothing's wrong
You make my short days feel so strong
Short days, long nights
But you make everything feel right

Serenity

In stillness lies a silent power
A gentle force, like a summer shower
It whispers softly in our ear
Inviting us to let go of fear

The world is rushing, chaos abounds
But in this moment, peace surrounds
Birds chirp a lullaby so sweet
As we sit and rest our weary feet

The rustling leaves, a soothing sound
Nature's beauty all around
It lulls us to a tranquil place
A haven for the human race

Oh, serenity, how you do heal
A balm for wounds that we can feel
Our souls take flight in your embrace
And feel the calm of your warm grace

May we seek you out in times of stress
And find solace in your caress
For in this world where chaos reigns
Serenity, your peace sustains.

Tranquil

Tranquil, oh tranquil, calm and serene
A peacefulness that cannot be seen
But felt within your very soul
A sense of calm that makes you whole

The rustle of leaves and gentle breeze
The sound of water that softly teases
A feeling of stillness, a sense of peace
A moment in time that will never cease

Tranquil, oh tranquil, a state of grace
Where worries and troubles have no trace
A place of refuge for the weary heart
A refuge where peace and joy can start

Tranquil, oh tranquil, a cherished prize
A moment where you can close your eyes
And feel the beauty that surrounds
A moment where true contentment abounds

So let us treasure this state of being
This tranquil state that leaves us dreaming
And let us all find our own little piece
Of tranquil, where our souls can find release.

Calm

Oh, tranquil sea, how beautiful you be
With gentle waves that caress the shore
The soothing sound of your ebb and flow
A symphony that lulls my soul to pure repose

The quietude of a forest's embrace
The rustling of leaves, the chirping of birds
A symphony of nature that brings me peace
And whispers to my heart, "Let your worries cease"

Calm, an oasis in a world of unrest
A haven for the restless heart to find rest
In the stillness, I find my tranquility
And a calming balm for my soul's fragility

So, let me dwell in this serene abode
And let my heart soar on the wings of peace
For in this realm of calmness my spirit comes alive
And I find my true self, at last, to thrive.

Mist

Mist, a veil of secrecy,
Falls upon the land so peacefully.
Its ethereal touch upon the trees,
Brings a sense of mystery and unease.

The world enveloped in a shroud,
As the mist descends like a cloud.
Trees once visible, now veiled,
As if secrets they've long held and never revealed.

The air is damp, chilled and calm,
A stillness, a pause, a moment of balm.
As if the earth herself is taking a break,
From the hustle and bustle of life-filled days.

The mist, a cloak-like embrace,
As if nature herself has a protective space.
A sense of magic, a mystical charm,
As if we're standing in the eye of the storm.

Mist, a natural wonder,
A mirage that makes the world ponder.
Its beauty and grace, a thing to behold,
A reminder of nature's power, wild and bold.

Gloomy

Gloomy clouds that blanket the sky,
Cloaking everything with their somber veil.
A heaviness lingers in the air,
As if the weight of the world is too much to bear.

The sun's light is stifled and subdued,
As if even it can't break through the gloom.
The world is dimmed by the murky haze,
And everything looks dull, mundane, and grey.

But amidst the murk, there's beauty to behold,
The dewdrops on petals, the mist on the fields.
The world seems to slow and become introspective,
As the clouds invite us to a moment of reflection.

And in this moment, we realize,
That gloom is but a fleeting emotion.
It teaches us to look deeper within,
And to cherish the moments of sunny commotion.

So embrace the gloom and all it brings,
Let it be the catalyst for deeper things.
For in the gloom, we can find beauty and light,
And learn to shine even in the darkest of nights.

Arcane

In the depths of the unknown,
Arcane secrets lie alone.
Whispers of magic, unheard
Mysteries to be unearthed.

With each incantation and spell,
The mysteries of the arcane realm,
Unfurl like the petals of a flower
Each petal a unique power.

The arcane is a river of hope,
Leading to untold discovery,
An elusive essence beyond scope,
A curious mix of magic and mystery.

With a touch of the arcane,
The elements become one,
All is balanced, in peace,
Under the light of the sun.

Oh, Arcane! how powerful thy name,
A source of magic, a fountain of flame
A mystical ecstasy that ignites,
A potent spell that never fades.

Pursuit

To pursue is to chase,
To strive for what we desire,
To never lose sight of the race,
To fuel the flames of our fire.

We seek our heart's desire,
With passion and fortitude,
Our minds set on the prize,
Our hearts beating with gratitude.

The path may be uncertain,
With obstacles in our way,
But we push on with determination,
With courage that will not sway.

For in the pursuit of our dreams,
We find strength we never knew,
We discover our hidden potential,
And all we can become anew.

So let us never give up the chase,
But pursue with all our might,
For in the end, it's not the prize we seek,
But the journey and the fight.

Occult

In the shadows of the night,
Lurks a world beyond our sight.
Mysteries we can't explain,
Whispers of the arcane.

The Occult, a realm untold,
A place where secrets unfold.
For those who dare to seek,
Mystery and wonder they'll meet.

The veil between worlds ever thin,
The unknown beckons us in.
A place where spirits roam,
And magic finds its home.

The power of the unseen,
A force that's not so clean.
For the Occult is a dark path,
That can lead to madness and wrath.

So tread with caution, if you will,
Into the Occult, a place that can thrill.
For the mysteries that await,
Can stir your soul and alter your fate.

Possessed

A demon dwells within me
It lurks beneath the skin
A haunting presence that devours
My sanity within

It whispers wicked secrets
And screams with bloody rage
A monstrous force that grips me tight
And never will disengage

It moves like fire through my veins
And leaves me so undone
I am a slave to its demands
A hostage to this one

How I wish to banish it
And make it go away
But it seems to know my every move
And refuses to obey

So now I learn to live with it
And try to keep it calm
For if I let it free to roam
It will do me only harm

Possessed I am, and yet I fight
To hold on to my light
For though it's dark and full of fright
I shall not lose the fight

Grove

In Groves of green and gold,
Lies a land so pure and bold,
Where nature speaks in a tongue untold,
And the birdsong echoes in the fold.

The trees rise high, their branches stretch,
Reaching up to the sky, almost to catch,
The essence of life, so pure and true,
In a land that's old and yet so new.

Here, the breeze whispers secrets untold,
As the leaves rustle, in union they behold,
The magic of life that's all around,
In a place that's serene and profound.

The grove is a place of peace and calm,
Amidst the chaos, it's a healing balm,
A resting place for the weary soul,
Where one can find solace, and be made whole.

In this grove of dreams and hope,
Where the heart and soul can truly cope,
Is a sanctuary for the wandering mind,
A place of serenity, hope and kind.

So come, dear friend, let's take a stroll,
In this grove where the mysteries roll,
And let our minds be free to roam,
In the land where the spirit finds a home.

Nether

Nether, land of mystery and fear
A world beneath where darkness veers
Where time is lost and shadows dwell
And echoes whisper secrets to tell

Tunnels winding, endlessly deep
The dark and dampness weaves its keep
The stalactites and stalagmites glow
Guiding wanderers to and fro

Creatures lurking in the abyss
Their presence sensed, not seen amiss
The echos grow louder, louder still
And fear begins to seep and spill

But Nether is not just a land of fright
It's a world of treasures, waiting in sight
Diamonds, gold and lapis too
A treasure trove, for those who pursue

So heed my words, oh traveler of might
Nether has both, darkness and light
Stepping forth requires fiery heart
To decipher Nether's secrets, an art.

Aquila

In the sky, so high and serene,
Where the clouds and the stars convene,
Aquila, the mighty eagle, flies,
His wings spreading wide, untied.

Majestic and proud, he soars,
Over mountains and canyons, he explores,
His piercing gaze scanning the land,
For prey to catch with his steadfast hand.

A symbol of freedom, courage, and grace,
Aquila inspires us to find our own place,
To spread our wings and take flight,
To be fierce and unyielding in our fight.

Aquila, the king of the sky,
His spirit, forever soaring high,
May his legend live on for all time,
A beacon of strength and a symbol divine.

Cloak

Cloak, a garment of mystery and grace,
A shroud of darkness for the hidden face,
An elusive veil that conceals the truth,
A symbol of power, a sign of youth.

Enigmatic and alluring, it swoops and swirls,
A protector of secrets, a shield from the world,
A shield that grants solace to those in pain,
A comfort to wear, it shields from the rain.

It conceals the scars of past pain,
It erases the tears and hides the stain,
It holds the promise of a future bright,
And protects us from the darkest night.

Cloak, oh mysterious and beautiful shroud,
Your presence leads us through any crowd,
You cloak us with a supernatural might,
And give us the strength to face the fight.

Flames

Flames dance, they flicker bright
With warmth and light and pure delight
Their beauty in the night so fierce
A mesmerizing, captivating sight

Each flame its own unique tale
Of passion, love, and even pain
Burning bright, then fading fast
Like memories, they come and go again

Flames can be both friend and foe
A force to both create and destroy
The warmth, the heat, the glow
Can leave us feeling both amazed and overjoyed

So let us all embrace the flames
And feel their magic in our souls
For they have the power to inspire
And ignite our passions, make us whole.

Elven

In the woods so deep and fair,
Where light and shadow blend in air,
A race of creatures, slim and tall,
Dance to the beat of nature's call.

Elven kind, graceful and pure,
Beneath the starry sky so sure,
With voices soft, like gentle breeze,
Their melodies put hearts at ease.

Their eyes as bright as forest dew,
With ancient wisdom shining through,
In timeless quests, they lead the way,
And guide us towards the light of day.

Their magic heals, their touch divine,
Their loyalty, forever fine,
In Elven lands, we find it all,
A realm of beauty, free from gall.

So heed their words, and listen well,
For life with them, is nothing but swell,
With Elven kind, we are one,
And nature's song, forever sung.

Enchanted

In the forest, where the trees stood tall
And the leaves whispered secrets to all
A hush came over the enchanted land
And we felt the magic's gentle hand

The breeze danced with the leaves
As the sun filtered through the eaves
The flowers bloomed, the bees hummed
Nature's symphony had begun

Oh, the beauty of the enchantment
As we were lost in the moment
The world around us fell away
And we felt our worries start to sway

For in this enchanted place
All troubles vanished without a trace
We basked in nature's harmony
And felt at peace with our reality

Oh, how joyous it was to see
How enchanted life could be
The magic of this precious land
Forever etched in our hearts and hands.

Totem

Totem, oh Totem, standing tall and proud
A beacon of heritage, a story to be told aloud
Carved with care, by hands skilled and wise
A symbol of culture that never dies

Each figure etched, holds a sacred meaning
A lineage of ancestors, each one gleaming
With wisdom and power, they stand as one
A testament to a time long gone

The bear, the wolf, the eagle too
Each one holds a significance true
A bonding of spirits, a calling of the wild
A reminder of our roots, like a precious child

So let us honor the Totem, with all our hearts
A tribute to our heritage, never to be torn apart
A symbol of unity, of respect and love
A shining light, sent from above.

Seal

Beneath the waves, there is a mystery,
A creature with a soul, so wild and free,
It glides with grace, through depths unknown,
A seal, a wonder, on its own.

Its eyes so deep, they draw you in,
A hint of mischief, a playful grin,
It moves with fluidity, a dance in the sea,
The seal, a picture of vitality.

Though hunted for its fur, it endures with might,
A survivor, a symbol of life's fight,
May we cherish this wonder, this creature so rare,
The seal, a legend, for all to share.

Psychic

Beyond the veil of mortal sight,
Lies a gift of untold might.
A power that can pierce the veil,
And see beyond the earthly pale.

A psychic's mind is like a lens,
That focuses on what lies within.
The thoughts and feelings we often hide,
Are laid bare for them to find.

The future's secrets are revealed,
And past events are unsealed.
The present moment is made clear,
As they see what's drawing near.

With heightened senses, they can feel,
The energy that others conceal.
A touch, a whisper, a hidden sigh,
All laid bare to the psychic's eye.

Oh, how wondrous is this gift,
That can uplift and heal the rift,
Between the seen and unseen,
And bring comfort to those who keen.

So let us honor the psychic's art,
And the treasure they share with heart,
For they remind us of the spark,
That lights the way through the dark.

Charm

Charm, oh sweet and wondrous thing,
That makes our hearts skip and sing.
It is the sparkle in your eyes,
The way you speak and mesmerize.

Charm is more than just a smile,
It is a grace that lasts a while.
It is the way you walk and move,
The way you laugh and gently soothe.

Charm is a magic spell we cast,
To make a moment truly last.
It is the spark that lights the fire,
And fills our souls with true desire.

Charm is a power all its own,
A force that reaches to the bone.
It is the beauty of the heart,
And the gift that sets us apart.

So hold on tight to your own charm,
And let it shine all bright and warm.
For it is the gift that we give,
And the magic that lets us live.

Titan

In the space beyond our planet's reach,
A colossal body drifts and breeches,
A world of ice and methane seas,
A place distant, yet it still breathes.

Titan, a satellite of Saturn,
With veiled shrouds and thick curtains,
Obscuring secrets of its origin,
Forlorn with ancient dust and sin.

Beneath the orange skies and haze,
A harsh land seeks the sun's warm embrace,
Mountains that pierce and valleys that sprawl,
A landscape that echoes a primal call.

Perhaps in Titan's sequestered land,
An extraterrestrial story takes a stand,
A world sculpted by forces unknown,
Lost in the universe's endless roam.

And so we ponder and we dream,
Of Titan's secrets concealed and unseen,
A world that stirs the human soul,
And reminds us of our endless role.

Momento Mori

In every breath we take,
Reality must be faced.
For time is a thief we cannot escape,
Thus, every moment should be embraced.

The sands of time may slip away,
And with it, all our dreams may fray,
But we must remember, day by day,
That life is fleeting, and we cannot delay.

In the face of death, we see our fate,
Our mortality we cannot escape,
But let us live, before it's too late,
And leave a legacy that cannot be erased.

Momento Mori, a reminder to us all,
That we are mortal, and life is but a call,
So let us live, with purpose and with gall,
And make every second here worth it all.

Ascetic

With eyes closed and hands on chest,
He sits in peace, as the world just rests.
In renunciation, he finds his bliss,
As he cuts the ties that cause all the fuss.

The scars on his feet remind us all,
Of the path he tread to reach this call.
He gave up what most of us hold dear,
To find a truth that was crystal clear.

He lives a life that's simple and bare,
With no material things that he wants to wear.
His mind's a temple, his heart's a shrine,
In solitude, he savors the divine.

He has no craving for food or fame,
For him, peace is the ultimate aim.
He's a light, a guide, a saintly soul,
Whose presence makes us feel whole.

His life's a message for all to see,
That true happiness lies in being free.
Free from the bondages of material things,
Asceticism is the path to our wings.

So, in reverence, we bow to thee,
O ascetic, thy spirit sets us free.

Flicker

Flicker, oh Flicker, burning bright,
A flame that dances in the night.
Your gentle glow, so warm and kind,
Bringing comfort to weary minds.

Like a beacon, you guide our way,
Through darkness and the bleakest days.
Your flicker speaks of hope and grace,
A symbol of the human race.

You flicker with a steady beat,
A rhythm that we all can meet.
You shine ahead and light our path,
And lead us through life's aftermath.

Flicker, oh Flicker, never fade,
Continue to light up our way.
We'll follow you, wherever you go,
And like your flame, we'll always grow.

Havoc

Anarchy reigns, as chaos unfolds
And destruction has taken hold
Havoc wreaks its devastating toll
Ravaging all, a heartless goal

Like a storm that rages on
Leaving nothing undisturbed, gone
Its power and force, impossible to resist
A merciless force, impossible to dismiss

The flame that consumes everything in its path
Leaving behind only destruction, no aftermath
Its wrath knows no bounds, no end in sight
A force to be feared, a terror to fight

But amidst the chaos and the pain
There is an inexplicable beauty that remains
For in the ashes and the ruins, new life begins
A symbol of hope, of transformation, that wins

So let havoc have its moment of rage
For it will be overcome, it will age
And in its place, a new dawn will arise
A testament to the human spirit that never dies.

Penta-edged

Five sharp edges, gleaming bright,
Penta-edged, a wondrous sight,
With each edge a deadly blade,
An art of death, a master made.

A weapon of precision fine,
Deadly, swift, yet so divine,
In skilled hands, it strikes with ease,
A dance of death, a sight to please.

Yet not for violence alone it's made,
An emblem of strength and skill displayed,
A symbol of mastery and might,
A shining star in the warrior's sight.

So let each edge be honed to keen,
Let each move be swift, unseen,
For in the art of war and grace,
The penta-edged will find its place.

Prism

Oh, prism, how you gleam and glow,
A rainbow of colors, a splendid show.
You capture the light, breaking it down,
A kaleidoscope of beauty, nothing to frown.

Red, orange, yellow, and green,
Blue, indigo, and violet, a stunning scene.
The colors dance and play in the light,
A shimmering display, oh what a delight.

Each color has a story to tell,
A feeling, a mood, a tale to unveil.
Red is passion, orange is warmth,
Yellow is joy, green is growth.

Blue is peace, indigo is mystery,
Violet is wisdom, and so much history.
Oh, prism, you hold the key,
To unlock emotions, so vast and free.

Your beauty shines so bright,
A beacon of hope, a symbol of might.
Prism, you are a work of art,
A masterpiece, close to my heart.

Spell

With just a chant and a flick of the wrist,
A world of magic we can enlist.
A spell can bring both joy and strife,
And reignite the magic in our life.

It can turn a pumpkin into a carriage,
Or summon forth a dangerous barrage.
It can heal a wound or cure a curse,
Or unleash a power that never disperses.

A spell can transport us to another realm,
Where dragons lurk and wizards helm.
It can grant the wish of the purest heart,
Or tear a love apart.
It's a power that should be used with care,
For magic can be both beautiful and rare.
But with a wise and steady hand,
A spell can create a wonderland.

So let us wield this magic well,
For with it, stories and legends doth swell.
Let us speak the language of the arcane,
And embrace the power within our veins.

The Storm

The sky grows dim and gray,
A storm is on its way,
The air grows heavy and still,
As the clouds begin to spill.

The wind roars and howls,
The rain beats against the tiles,
The thunder crashes and booms,
As the lightning lights up the rooms.

The trees bend and sway,
As the storm has its way,
Nature's fury is unleashed,
As the storm can never be leashed.

But in the midst of the chaos,
There is something peaceful, almost,
As the storm rages on and on,
A sense of calmness is drawn.

For in the storm, we see,
The power of nature's majesty,
A reminder of the raw force,
That weaves through all things in course.

The storm may bring fear and fright,
But it also brings a sense of might,
A reminder of our place,
In this world of mystery and grace.

Timeless

What is timeless, but a moment that lasts forever?
A memory that never fades, a love that never withers.
It's the feeling of a summer breeze, the smell of autumn leaves,
The colors of a sunset, the sound of crashing waves.

Timeless is a treasure that we all seek to find,
A magic that defies the ticking of the hands of time.
It's a bond that knows no distance, a friendship that never ends,
The thought that lives on, past the grave and the bends.

It's a photograph that captures a moment so dear,
A melody that transports us to another hemisphere.
Timeless is a promise that we make with our hearts,
A legacy that we leave, through our passions and arts.

So let us cherish these moments, these fragments of eternity,
For they are the threads that make up the tapestry of humanity.
They are the memories we hold dear, the dreams we wish to pursue,
The timeless treasures that make life worth living, through and through.

Relic

In a place of forgotten treasures,
Lies a relic of times gone by.
A history enshrined in gold,
A mystery that makes us sigh.

Its shape is worn and weathered,
As if a hundred years have passed.
But its beauty still shines through,
A rare gem that will forever last.

Men have fought and died for it,
Oaths and promises made.
For this relic holds the key,
To a past that cannot be swayed.

Its secrets are locked away,
In hidden chambers none can find.
But the relic holds them all,
Memories and stories intertwined.

So let us gaze upon it,
This relic of a bygone age.
And let its beauty and power,
Fill our hearts with awe and sage.

For in this treasure we see,
A story of our own lives.
A journey through time and space,
A relic that forever survives.

Trickster

In the shadows and the light,
A figure dances with delight,
A Trickster born of cunning schemes,
And clever riddles and devious dreams.

He slips between the veil of time,
And dances through the world's sublime,
With a sly grin and a mischief-loose,
The Trickster sows his chaos through.

But do not fear the Trickster's call,
For he brings joy to one and all,
A force of nature, wild and free,
A reminder of the joys that be.

So dance with Trickster, if you will,
And let your heart dance and thrill,
For in his laughter and his jest,
The Trickster shows us life at its best.

The Witch Bane's Curse

In the shadows of the night,
A whisper echoes through the trees,
A curse that fills the heart with fright,
And brings the bravest man to his knees.

Witch Bane, they call her by name,
A fearsome sorceress of old,
With power to drive men insane,
And a heart cold as winter's snow.

She weaves her spells with darkness and fear,
And casts them on the unwary and bold,
With her wicked whispers in the ear,
Her victims' fate is sealed and foretold.

But beware, dear friend, of Witch Bane's spell,
For once it touches your heart,
It will morph into a living hell,
And tear your world apart.

So if you must venture into her domain,
Be sure to arm your heart with love,
For only then can you hope to maintain,
The strength to resist Witch Bane's Curse from above.

Apex

In Apex, the mighty towers rise,
Tall and proud against the skies.
A thriving city, bustling with life,
Where dreams are made and fortunes thrive.

From morning light to setting sun,
The streets are crowded, never done.
The people here are full of fire,
Working hard, their hearts in desire.

Amidst it all, there's beauty too,
The parks and lakes, the skies so blue.
Nature and progress coexist,
In Apex, a rare duet that persists.

Innovation, progress, and passion,
The city thrives on these three fashion.
A beacon of hope, an urban delight,
Apex, you fill us with joy and light.

So let us raise a toast to thee,
A city that's our destiny.
Apex, you're our shining star,
May your fortunes ever soar and far.

Arcanist

In the land of magic and mystery,
Where spells and incantations roam free,
There lived a wise and powerful mage,
Whose name echoed through every page.

His words were like a symphony,
A melody of arcane beauty,
His power could shake the very earth,
And bring a new magic to birth.

With every wave of his wand,
A new adventure would dawn,
And tales of his greatness spread far and wide,
Like a wildfire that could never subside.

And so the Arcanist, magician supreme,
Remains a fixture in every dream,
A symbol of magic's infinite possibilities,
And of the wonders that lie in its mysteries.

Shadows

In the stillness of the night,
When the moon is shining bright,
The world is draped in inky hues,
And shadows start to come in view.

They dance upon the walls and floor,
Whisper secrets we can't ignore,
They bring to life our deepest fears,
And remind us of the passing years.

For shadows follow every step,
And linger long after we've left,
They're a reminder of what was behind,
A trace of the past still on our mind.

But shadows aren't just darkness and gloom,
They can be comfort in an empty room,
A sign that there is light somewhere,
Just waiting for us to become aware.

So don't fear the shadows you see,
For they are part of you and me,
A reminder that we never stand alone,
And that even darkness has it's own light shown.

Fallen Sky

The sky was once a canvas vast,
A tapestry of blue that held fast.
But one day, it all came crashing down,
The heavens shattered, the world around.

The sun and stars, once shining bright,
Were snuffed out like a candle in the night.
The moon, no longer a guiding light,
Fell with a thud, upon the earth's might.

The birds that soared now lay below,
Their wings shattered, no longer aglow.
The planes that once roared across the sky,
Crashed down to earth, an eerie lullaby.

The world was changed, forever more,
Its skies darkened, its future unsure.
And yet, amidst the chaos and despair,
A flicker of hope, a glimmering flare.

For as the sky fell to the ground,
A new world was born, slowly unbound.
A world of wonder, of magic and might,
Where dreams take flight, even in the night.

So though the sky may be fallen and dead,
A new world of possibilities lies ahead.
For in every end, there is a new beginning,
And in every fall, a chance for winning.

Desolator

The Desolator stands tall, a towering sight
Its shadow dwarfs all in its might
A fearsome creature, like a demon from hell
Its very presence makes the bravest hearts quell

The Desolator ravages and destroys without care
Leaving nothing but ruins, despair, and despair
Its eyes glower like fire, its breath like a storm
All who see it quake, praying to be left unharmed

But amid the horror, there is a glimmer of light
A few brave souls still stand, ready to fight
They hold their ground, never giving in
Defying the Desolator, refusing to be beaten

For every wound, they inflict on the beast
One step closer they come to a victory feast
And when the Desolator falls, vanquished at last
Their hearts sing with triumph, the future no longer aghast

The Desolator, a symbol of terror and dread
But in the face of adversity, hope is still bred
For where there is darkness, there is always light
And where there is hope, there's always a chance to fight.

Elixir

Golden fluid brews,
Warming, soothing, healing touch,
Elixir divine.

Cherry blossoms sway,
Elixir's sweet fragrance fills,
Springtime in a sip.

Mandarin and mint,
Elixir's zesty essence,
Lightens up the soul.

Essence

Dew drops on petals,
Essence of morning captured,
Life's beauty revealed.

Soft whispers of wind,
Essence of nature's secrets,
Speak to my spirit.

Heart's essence revealed,
In simple acts of kindness,
Love's power expressed.

Faded

Colors once so bold,
Now washed out and hard to see,
Faded memories.

Sunset in the west,
Colors slowly disappear,
Nature fades to black.

Faded beauty,
Like leaves falling from a tree,
The circle of life.

Fusion

Nuclear forces merge
Infinite energy born
Fusion of the sun

Particles collide
Releasing intense power
Fusion ignites life

Fusing minds, ideas
Innovation at its peak
Creativity's blaze

Rune

Magical symbols
Etched in ancient stones and trees
Rune whispers secrets

Frosty northern land
Warriors carve divine words
Rune protects and guides

Mystery and myth
Rune unlocks the unseen realms
Wonders to behold

Faerie

Soft wings flutter by
Magical lands filled with light
Faerie realm awakes

Fluttering sprites dance
Gossamer wings catch the breeze
Joyful laughter rings

Faerie queen reigns supreme
Flowers bloom in her gentle wake
Majestic and wise

Undying

Death cannot claim me,
Eternal soul, undying,
Forever to be.

Immortal spirit,
Defying the hands of fate,
Undying and free.

Endless is my life,
Beyond the reach of the grave,
Undying always.

Illusionist

Tricks played on the eye,
Sleight of hand, a skilled deceit,
Illusionist's art.

Smoke and mirrors blend,
Magic fills the air with awe,
Illusionist's spell.

Mystery surrounds,
Illusionist leaves us stunned,
Wondering what's real.

Destruction

Nature's fury rages
Destruction in its wake leaves
Hope for new life sprouts

War's relentless march
Cities crumble under bombs
Peaceful homes now dust

Anger fueled actions
Rage and hate leave nothing but
Ruins and regret

Phoenix

Firebird takes flight
Rising from the ashes strong
Phoenix's rebirth

Heat of the desert
Wings spread wide in radiant flight
Phoenix's triumph

Eternal symbol
Everlasting flame of life
Phoenix, rise again

Ash

Ash in the fireplace
Dancing in the warm embrace
Winter's sweet solace

Forest burned to ash
Renewal begins from scrap
Phoenix from the ash

Ash of love letters
Destroyed but memories stay
Tears on old pages

Amulet

An amulet's charm,
Glimmers in the moonlit night,
Stay safe, my darling.

A mystical gem,
Warding off misfortune's surge,
Guardian divine.

Resilient talisman,
Protection from evil's grip,
Beacon of solace.

Jelly

Jiggling and wiggling,
Rainbow colors of delight,
Jelly brings me joy.

Sweet, glistening globes
Wrapped in a transparent sheen,
Jelly is divine.

Juicy fruit essence
Set in a quivering mass,
Jelly satisfies.

Leveller

Revolution comes
Equality for all men
Levellers arise

None are above law
Leveller's justice prevails
Freedom for all folks

No lord over me
A new order will arise
Leveller's demand

Third Eye

The third eye opens,
Knows secrets beyond the veil,
Intuition guides.

Mystical beacon,
Third eye leads to inner peace,
Awareness awakes.

The third eye sees all,
Deep knowledge and visions flow,
Soul's journey unfolds.

Tome

Tome, the wise old book
Pages full of knowledge deep
Endless tales to seek

Tome, an ancient guide
Lost secrets of forgotten times
Eternally resides

Tome, a heavy weight
Knowledge on every page held
Power to create

Aghanim

Aghanim, the mage
Master of the ancient arts
Power beyond dreams

His staff lights the way
Through the darkness of the night
Aghanim's great skill

Fight with wisdom's might
With Aghanim's guidance gained
Victory we claim

Trident

Trident, ocean king
In its hands lies untold power
Majestic beauty

Underwater world
Trident guards secrets unknown
Peaceful, yet deadly

Trident, godly force
Protector of the unknown
Mystery and might

Vampire

Eyes red as blood drops,
Fangs sharp as silver needles,
Vampire haunts the night.

Pale skin, frozen heart,
Lifeless form, yet full of lust,
Vampire longs for love.

Seductive beauty,
Immortal thirst never quenched,
Vampire's fatal charm.

Witless

A mind lost in fog,
Wisdom and wit beyond reach,
Witless wandering soul.

Empty words and deeds,
Witless actions, hollow thoughts.
Barren, bleak and cold.

Mirthless, humorless,
Nothing but a dull gray life,
Witless existence.

Striders

Silent as a breeze,
Striders glide through marshy reeds-
Nature's wondrous steeds.

Long legs stretch with ease,
Proud Striders grace the water,
Graceful and serene.

In the morning mist,
Striders wade in still waters,
A sight to behold.

Dimensional

A portal opens
A new world for us to see
Dimensional shift

Colors blend and blur
Realities intertwine
Dimensional waves

Boundless perspectives
Futuristic dreams come true
Dimensional realm

Doorway

A wooden portal,
Welcomes me with open arms,
Home sweet home awaits.

In a room alone,
A portal to another world,
Doorway to escape.

Creaking with each step,
An eerie door to nowhere,
Fear grips my soul tight

Horizon

Endless stretch ahead,
Colors blend into the sky,
Horizon in sight.

Sun dips down to sleep,
Silhouette horizon line,
Day and night complete.

Sky and sea as one,
Whidbey Island on the horde,
Tranquility found.

Fortitude

With fortitude strong,
Difficulties won't last long.
Peace will come erelong.

Endurance and grit,
A warrior's heart and wit.
Fortitude so fit.

With courage in hand,
Fortitude makes one withstand
Challenges so grand.

Satchel

Furry friend with paws,
Brings joy with every waggle,
Satchel, we love you.

Golden coat shines bright,
Running free across the fields,
Oh, Satchel, you thrill.

Loyal to his pack,
Guardian of the homestead,
Satchel, our true friend.

Vengeance

Aching to repay,
injustice incites revenge,
poison to the soul.

Eye for an eye, law
of vengeance, a bloody path,
ends in emptiness.

Vengeance breeds anger,
fury ignites the fire within,
leaves us consumed, lost.

Star

Stars twinkle at night
Guiding us through the darkness
Hope in the cosmos

Starlight, star bright
First star I see tonight
Wish I may, wish I might

Ethereal light
Cosmic fires blaze in space
Majestic star, shine

Mace

A mace in his hand
An ancient weapon of steel
Powerful and grand

Silent guardian brought
To defend the kingdom's gate
The mace stands alone

Heavy burden borne
Mace of justice, law, and might
Guiding hand of truth

Venom

Slithering serpent,
Poisonous fangs strike deadly,
Venomous demise.

Black and white attire,
Vicious tongue drips toxic words,
Venomous villain.

Lurking in shadows,
Venomous eyes gleam with greed,
Waiting to strike prey.

Warhammer

Amidst battlefield,
Warriors wield weapons with skill,
Chaos reigns supreme.

In grim darkness, fight,
Warriors of Imperium,
Emperor's light shines.

Blood for the Blood God,
Khorne's followers seek battle,
Skulls adorn their path.

Clarity

Crystal clear water
I see my reflection, pure
Clarity of self

Mind a tranquil sea
No piercing thought can disturb
Clear, serene, focused

Morning air so crisp
Sun beams through a prism's grace
Clarity shines bright

Deceit

False words on his lips,
Hidden intentions beneath,
Deceit's cunning plan.

Eyes that feign the truth,
Deceptive smile on his face,
Deceitful man's guise.

Hollow promises,
Secrets lurking in the dark,
Deceit's wicked grip.

Enchanted

A world of wonder,
Enchanted forest awaits,
Nature's magic charm.

Whispers in the wind,
Heartbeats of the mystic woods,
Enchanted silence.

Fairytales come true,
With every step enchanted,
A dreamland in view.

Shard

A silent giant,
Stretching toward the heavens high,
Shard pierces the sky.

Jagged edges gleam,
Glistening in the sunlight,
Crystal shard aflame.

Atop the skyline,
A shard of glass stands alone,
Dominating all.

Circlet

Circle of metal
Circlet crowns a queen's head high
Regal grace exudes

Tiny jewels abound
On the delicate circlet
Sparkling starry night

Silver or gold bands
Worn in ancient mythology
Circlet still shines bright

Magi

Magi, wise and true
Guided by starlight, they pursue
A journey of faith, a journey of hope
A journey that led them to Christ's abode

Their gifts they brought, rich and rare
Humble offerings, filled with care
Gold for a King, frankincense for a Priest
Myrrh for the One who'd suffer and cease

Magi, wise and brave
Their story etched in time, a treasure to save
They sought the truth, they found the light
In a manger, on a holy night

Their example, still relevant today
To seek the divine, to find our way
Magi, a timeless symbol of faith
Their legacy, an eternal grace.

Alacrity

With Alacrity, I rise to meet the day
A fire in my spirit, ablaze in every way
My heart imbued with boundless zeal
A thirst for life that cannot be still

I leap into the fray with joyful haste
A warrior's heart, with no time to waste
I dance a merry dance with life
A partner in the grandest strife

And as I move, with Alacrity abound
My eyes are drawn to beauty all around
An endless field of flowers at my feet
A marvel I cannot help but greet

And so I run, with Alacrity pure
A soul reborn, forevermore
For in this haste, I find great peace
A freedom from the mundane, an endless feast.

Wizardry

Oh, magic in your fingertips
A world of wonder, at your grip
Words and spells, a symphony
Of wonders wrought, in secrecy

Through ancient tomes and incantations
Of power, born of all creations
A wizard's wand, with sparks ablaze
A universe of sorcery, a dreamy daze

A flash of light, and a burst of flame
A binding spell, or a summoning name
A force of nature that bends to will
With secrets whispered, and purest skill

Oh, wizardry, a spell so rare
A world of sorcery, beyond compare
With powers brightly shining bright
A world of magic, come to light

Quelling

In the midst of chaos and strife
When tempers flare and minds are blind
Comes a force that can calm the storm
A power that's gentle yet so refined

It's the art of quelling, the calm within
A balm for wounds that rage and fester
When anger boils and hate commands
A soothing touch can bring peace, no pressure

It's the voice that speaks to quell the rage
The hand that halts the fist mid-flight
It's the heart that harbors empathy
And the love that sheds a healing light

For in the end, it's not the might that wins
Nor the words that cut like a knife
It's the grace that flows from within
That has the power to change a life

So let us learn the art of quelling
And the power of a gentle touch
For in this world of chaos and strife
We need it now more than ever, so much.

Infused Raindrops

As I look up into the sky,
I see the raindrops falling by,
Each of them a precious gift,
To bring new life and spirits lift.

Infused with grace and magic rare,
They come to heal, to soothe, to care,
And in their gentle, misty touch,
They cleanse the earth with love so much.

They wash away the tears and pain,
And bring the hope of sun again,
For in each drop, there lies a prayer,
That all may find the love we share.

So when you see the raindrops fall,
Know they are more than just a squall,
For in each drop, there is a spark,
Of life, of love, of hope and stark.

And though the storm may rage on high,
The rain will come to renew and fly,
For in each drop, there lies a dream,
That all may find the love they deem.

Venom

Venomous fangs, dripping with hate
A deadly substance, a poison to fate
It strikes without warning, without care
A silent killer, lurking everywhere

An insidious force, it spreads and grows
Attacks the heart, the mind, the soul
It corrupts your thoughts, it clouds your mind
A venomous serpent, a destroyer of kind

Like an invisible demon, it twists and turns
An uncontrollable force, it forever churns
It feeds on anger, fear, and resentment
A venomous infection, without an ointment

So be wary of this venomous foe
A force that haunts, a force that won't let go
For in its grasp, it will drag you down
And leave you lost, with no way to be found.

Blight

A disease on the land,
A tragedy for all to see,
The blight that grows and spreads,
A curse on society.

Fields once lush with life,
Now barren wastelands stand,
A testament to devastation,
A harsh and bitter brand.

The rust and rot of blight,
A marking on the earth,
A sign of pain and sorrow,
A deep and lasting hurt.

Yet in the midst of this despair,
A spark of hope appears,
A light that shines within the dark,
Banishing all fears.

For though the blight may linger,
And the damage may remain,
The heart of nature beats strong,
And love will always reign.

So let us not succumb to despair,
Nor let our souls be bowed,
For in the midst of blight,
Hope and love can still be found.

Blitz

The sirens wail with a mournful scream,
As darkness falls upon the city scene.
The Blitz has come and terror reigns,
As bombs fall from the sky like fiery rains.

Buildings crumble and homes are lost,
Families scatter at an unforgiving cost.
The air is thick with smoke and dust,
A ghostly mist that only adds to the disgust.

But amidst this chaos and destruction,
A spirit rises up, a fierce production.
The people of this land will never rest,
Until their homes are once again at their best.

For the Blitz may rage on with all its might,
But it will never conquer this nation's fight.
With unity and courage they will stand,
Defying the darkness with a steadfast hand.

So let the sirens scream and bombs fall,
For the people of this land will never crawl.
Their spirit unyielding and hearts so strong,
They will rise above and carry on.

Mithril

Mithril, a metal of legends,
Forged in fires of silver and godly ore,
A precious alloy that shines with beauty,
And hardness that no other can boast.

From the mountains of Middle-earth,
Comes Mithril, beyond measure and worth,
A gift of the earth to the wise and brave,
For only the ones with pure hearts will save.

In the darkness of Mines of Moria,
The Dwarves found Mithril, a glorious treasure,
It sparkled like stars in the dark,
Hope for their quest, a light in their hearts.

The Elves, the Men, and Dwarves all knew
That Mithril held secrets that true,
In their armors and weapons they used,
Mithril proved to be unmatched and fused.

Now, tales of Mithril live on,
In songs that tell of heroes long gone,
A metal that stands the test of time,
Mithril, forever a treasure divine.

Sage

Sage, oh Sage, with leaves so green,
Aromatic herb of wisdom seen,
Drawing out memories profound,
Cleansing spirits that surround.

In teas and dishes, you appear,
A versatile leaf in every sphere,
Your essence brings healing power,
Calming nerves in any hour.

Oh Sage, with ancient roots,
You've shared the world with many fruits,
Your presence always felt so true,
In our hearts, we turn to you.

Guiding us through trails and paths,
You teach us how to live and laugh,
With you, we find our center,
And peace within, we enter.

Oh Sage, with branches so wide,
Encompassing all that we abide,
With your energy, we strive to rise,
And soar to greater heights and prize.

So let us honor you, Oh Sage,
For all the blessings you impart,
May your essence continue to grace,
And inspire us with your heart.

Fluffy

Oh, Fluffy! Your coat so soft and fine
Is like a cloud from heaven divine
A purr that sings a melodic tune
A heart that shines like the fullest moon

Your eyes like pearls, so bright and round
Reflecting love and joy that abound
A soul that's pure, a spirit that's free
A noble being, loyal as can be

In your presence, worries cease to be
A simple touch, and I feel so carefree
Your furry body, like a warm embrace
A tranquil haven, a joyous place

Oh, Fluffy! You bring me such delight
A faithful friend, a beacon of light
May your purrs and playful frolics
Fill our days with love and magic!

Morbid

There's darkness in the Morbid
A shadow that consumes
The air around you thickens
As the power of morbidity looms

It whispers sinister secrets
And feeds on your fears
The more you try to escape it
The closer it appears

Morbid is the echo
Of every sorrowful cry
It's the unrelenting pressure
That never seems to die

But among the shadows
There's a glimmer of light
A hope that shines so fierce
It banishes the Morbid into the night

So when the Morbid threatens
And the darkness descends
Look for the flicker of hope
And let it be your friend.

Amulet

A charm against the fates,
A symbol of protection,
A talisman to allay our fears,
The amulet is our ally.

It holds our hopes,
And guards against our doubts,
A reminder of all that is good,
And a shield against all that is bad.

Like a compass to the lost,
It shows us the way,
And guides us through life's storms.

For in its cool embrace,
We find sanctuary,
A haven of peace,
A refuge of solace.

So hold tight,
To your amulet,
And let its magic,
Guide your steps,
Through the uncertainty of life.

Blink

Blink, the moment so quick,
Fleeting and ephemeral, oh so slick.
It comes and goes in the blink of an eye,
A fleeting moment we cannot deny.

Blink, the pause that gives us space,
A moment to breathe and find our place.
It's a chance to stop and look around,
And see the beauty that's often profound.

In the blink, we find a moment of peace,
A chance to let our worries cease.
We can let go of all that's past,
And in the present, we can truly last.

So don't underestimate the power of a blink,
It's a moment that can make us think.
It reminds us to slow down and see,
All the wonders that are meant to be.

Void

The void lies before me
Endless, deep and dark
A place of unknown secrets
Where the lost souls embark

It's a place where nothing exists
No light, no sound, no air
An endless expanse of nothingness
A place of deep despair

The void calls out to me
A tempting, haunting call
But I know what will happen
If I let myself fall

For once you're in the void
It's impossible to be free
Forever trapped in nothingness
For all eternity

The void may call my name
But I'll resist its siren song
For I'll never let it claim me
And hold me for too long

Even in the darkest depths
Of the void's endless expanse
I choose to find the light
And take a chance

Talisman

Talisman, oh Talisman,
A symbol of luck and power,
Intriguing and mysterious,
Glistening in the midnight hour.

It holds within its polished stone,
A secret story yet untold,
Of ancient wisdom, magic spells,
And sorrows too hard to behold.

With colors deep and vivid hues,
A sight to make the heart rejoice,
It dances in the summer breeze,
And sings with the angels' voice.

Talisman, oh Talisman,
A treasure that we all seek,
To bring us love and happiness,
And make our dreams come to peak.

So hold it close and cherish it,
This magical piece you now own,
For who knows what the future brings,
And what seeds it has sown.

Talisman, oh Talisman,
A beacon in the dark,
A light that guides us through the storms,
And leaves an eternal mark.

Evasion

It's easy to pretend and lie,
Hide our truth and never try,
To speak the words that we deny,
And evade what's difficult to imply.

Sometimes it's fear that makes us hide,
Afraid of what we'll feel inside,
So we run away and try to bide,
Time until the fear subsides.

We all have parts that we evade,
Memories that we try to shade,
So we don't have to feel the pain,
Or that truth we cannot sustain.

But someday the wall we build will fall,
And all those secrets will be called,
Evasion no longer can be called,
For the truth will set us free after all.

Mystic

In the heart of the unknown, where eternal whispers roam
A place where magic reigns and the veil is never blown
The mystic calls, her voice a haunting melody
A fathomless beauty that captures the heart of many

With eyes as deep as the ocean, and a stare that pierces the soul
The mystic reveals the secrets of life, and the mysteries she unfolds
Her essence is enigmatic, and her words are captivating
With each verse, she takes us on a journey that's exhilarating

She speaks of love and loss, of dreams and desires
Of the boundless wonders of the universe, and the stars that inspire
She reveals the truth of our existence, and the beauty in our flaws
She shows that life is a tapestry, woven by countless laws

In the heart of the unknown, where the mystic dwells
The answers to our deepest questions reside in her spells
So let us listen, with open hearts and open minds
To the mystic's timeless wisdom, and the magic she entwines.

Reaver

Reaver, oh elusive one,
a heart as dark as coal,
a soul that's lost its sun,
a spirit that's lost control.

Every step you take,
leaves a trail of dread,
every move you make,
fills people with dread.

A pirate on the seas,
a thief in the night,
a shadow that flees,
with every stroke of light.

Your heart is full of malice,
your mind a twisted maze,
every deed a callous,
that leaves the world ablaze.

But still we cannot help,
but feel a sense of awe,
for despite your moral wealth,
you've a charisma that leaves us raw.

So here's to you Reaver,
may your legend never die,
may your spirit never waver,
as you ride into the void of night sky.

Sacred

The world is awash with beauty,
The mystery of creation is woven within,
Infinite wonders and marvels,
Beyond the depth of human sin.

We look up to the heavens,
And lo! we behold the sacred,
A divinity so great and awesome,
Invisible but deeply embedded.

The essence of life flows and glows,
All things that exist are in His hands,
Can you see the love and compassion,
Mirroring the light of His holy strands.

The sacred power of love and grace,
That nurtures the earth and the sky,
The pulse of life and its rhythms,
In His presence we learn to rely.

Thus, let us lift our hands and hearts,
From the depths of our innermost being,
To honor and worship the sacred,
The beginning and end of all seeing.

Wraith

A shadowy being that haunts the night,
With eyes that gleam like spectral light,
Wraith, oh wraith, how do you thrive,
In a world that cannot see you move or strive?

Your cloak it billows with a lifeless wind,
Your form is translucent, an ethereal kind,
Do you seek revenge, or just to haunt,
To chill the living, and make them daunt?

Wraith, oh wraith, you are enigmatic,
A being of darkness, and fearsome magic,
You linger in forgotten places,
Leaving traces of your eerie faces.

Do you find solace in the world you haunt,
Or do you long for a brighter dawn?
Do you seek to find redemption,
Or are you but a mere apparition?

Wraith, oh wraith, you mystify,
A specter ever present, always nearby,
Your legends persist through the ages,
Whispered in hushed tones, echoes in ancient pages.

Forevermore you shall reign,
A haunting figure of ghostly pain,
Wraith, oh wraith, forevermore,
Your secrets kept forevermore.

Death

Of all life's truths, the end we cannot flee,
A path we each must tread, without reprieve,
The fading light of mortal certainty,
That bids us come to terms with our reprieve.
For death is not an end, but just the start,
A passage to a place beyond our sight,
Where loved ones rest, and souls are held apart,
From mortal coils that bind within our might.
In dying, we achieve a state of peace,
No longer bound by earthy concerns,
A time of rest, where all our struggles cease,
And we may finally lay down our concerns.
So let us not fear death Nor dread the day,
For though it comes, it but leads us onward's way.

Fate

Fate, an unseen force that guides our way
A destiny that shapes our path each day
It draws us to the places we belong
And reveals to us where we belong
With each decision, fate is at our side
It whispers in our ear, a gentle guide
And though we may protest and may resist
We find that fate was right, and we persist
It can be kind or cruel, this force of fate
A burden that we bear, a weight
It can snatch away our dreams, our hopes
And leave us with despair and endless slopes
But still, we cling onto fate's strong hand
Trusting it will lead us to the promised land
For deep within our hearts, we know it's true
That fate will never steer us wrong, or lead us to rue
So, let us embrace our destiny with grace
And trust that fate will guide us to the right place.

Gone

A couch already forgotten
Memories in the foam
Hearts were spilled out
Too many a moments
The sunsets and the moon
Not a soul in the room
Everything whispers
But all's being dragged
Towards yesterday

Without You

What am I without you, my love?
A restless soul, a bird without a nest
A heart that flutters, lost without its dove
A life that's incomplete, unfulfilled at best Without you, colors fade to
gray
The world's a darker, dreary place
Where once was light, it's gone away
And left me with an emptiness to face
Your essence lingers like a dream
Of the person I was when you were near
But even in your absence, I know
That love endures, and that you're always here
A whisper on the breeze, a memory
A transcending love that's evergreen
Forever etched within my heart, a legacy Without you, I'm but a shadow
So I'll cherish what we had, my love
And keep it close, like a precious jewel
Forever in my heart, you'll always be enough The perfect match, the
missing piece, the guiding fuel

Fade Into You

As I lay my head down to sleep,
I think of you and how you sweep
All my fears and doubts away
Your voice and touch, forever stay
I close my eyes and I can see
Your face before me, so clearly
The way you smile and laugh and sing
The warmth you bring, the joy you bring
And as the night falls and the world fades
I feel your love, like a gentle wave
That carries me, and I fade into you
Lost in your embrace, I find my truth
With you, I am complete, I am whole
You are the source of my very soul
So let me stay here, in this moment true
Fade into you, and never let go.

Help Me

I'm lost,
I'm scared,
My path is unclear,
I'm drowning,
I'm suffocating,
In a life that's filled with fear.
The weight of the world,
It's all on my shoulders,
I'm struggling to keep up,
To keep my head above the waters.
My heart is heavy,
With the burden I bear,
I'm crying out for help,
But it feels like no one's there.
In the darkness of the night,
I cry myself to sleep,
Longing for someone to hold my hand,
To guide me through the deep.
So please, won't you help me,
Won't you light my way,
I promise to hold on tight,
And never let go astray.
For in your strength and love,
I find the courage to fight,
To face the storm head-on,

And come out on the other side.

Into The Mystic

Into the mystic we go,
A journey that few will know,
With the wind as our guide,
And the stars as our show.
We sail across the sea,
In search of a place to be,
Where the moon meets the sun,
And the sound of waves is free.
Into the mystic, we find,
A world that's both pure and kind,
Where love and peace abide,
And all worries are left behind.
And the air is full of thunder,
As we dance to the rhythm,
Of the universe's plunder.
Into the mystic, we venture,
With our hearts and souls as center,
The land is full of wonder,
And we emerge anew,
With a sense of peace that's forever.
So if you seek a journey,
Where the unknown is worthy,
Take my hand and let's go,
Into the mystic, so otherworldly.

No Ordinary Love

No ordinary love do I feel,
A flame that burns eternal and real.
A passion that fills me to the brim,
A love that knows no bounds or dim.
For this love is more than just desire,
It's a force that no one can quench or tire.
It's a love that's pure and free of chains,
A love that endures all the pains.
Through storms and trials, it stands strong,
A love that forever will belong.
To hearts that beat with the same tune,
This love is a treasure, a priceless boon.
No ordinary love do I hold,
It's worth more than any precious gold.
It's a love that's rare and one of a kind,
A love that's divine, it's hard to find.
So I'll cherish it with all my heart,
And from it, I'll never be apart.
For this love is what makes life worth living,
A love that's everlasting and giving.

I Can't Stand The Rain

I can't stand the rain,
It falls like shards of pain,
Each drop a reminder,
Of things I can't find a reminder,
It's a lonely and cold weather,
With a rhythm that never falters,
It pounds the rooftop and the ground,
Echoing the sorrows that abound.
The rain brings memories,
Of love that once danced to this breeze,
So I close my eyes and reminisce,
As I kiss the pain with each mist.
I know that hope can keep me warm,
But even in the midst of the storm,
So I let the rain wash me clean,
And start afresh like a dream.
For I know that after the rain,
The sun will invariably reign,
And I'll bask in its golden glow,
Leaving all my sorrows below.

If I Ain't Got You

If I ain't got you, my heart weeps
Like a sky without any stars
Like a river without any fish
Like a garden without any flowers
If I ain't got you, life is dull
Like a canvas with no colors
Like a melody with no sound
Like a story with no ending
You are the sunshine in my day
The moonlight in my night
The warmth in my soul
The reason to fight
Without you, everything fades
Joy and happiness become shades
Life seems incomplete and hollow
But with you, my soul follows
So hold my hand, never let go
Together we'll face the world and grow
With you, my heart feels complete
If I ain't got you, my heart skips a beat.

Passionate Kisses

Passionate kisses, a flame that ignites
A connection so deep, a feeling so raw
A moment of heat, an electric sight
A bond that's created, beyond any flaw
The touch of your lips, a sweet, lingering taste As your arms wrap around
me, a loving embrace
As The intense desire that fills up the air
A passionate kiss, a moment so rare
In this kiss, I feel alive
A spark that sets forth, and thrives
A passion that cannot be tamed
A fire that cannot be blamed
In the midst of a passionate kiss,
My heart swells up, my soul with bliss
An explosion of love, a wave of affection
A bond that's unbreakable, beyond all perception
Passionate kisses, a force so true
A feeling that's shared, between me and you
As our lips touch, we become one
A union full of love, a bond that won't be undone.

I Miss You

I miss the warmth of your embrace,
The touch of your hand on my face,
I miss your laughter and your smile,
The way you made every moment worthwhile. I miss the sound of your
voice,
The way you made my heart rejoice,
I miss the love that we shared,
Everything about you,
I have always cared.
The days are long and cold without you,
My heart aches for your touch so true,
I miss the way you held me tight,
Making everything feel just right.
Oh, how I long to see your face,
To feel the warmth of your embrace,
Until that day when we meet anew,
I will keep missing you.

Follow You

*I'll follow you, my love, wherever you may go Through mountains high or
valleys low
I'll be your guide, your faithful friend
I'll walk with you through storm and rain
And hold your hand through all the pain
Until the very end I'll never leave,
I'll always stay
By your side come what may
For you are the light that makes my heart shine The love that warms this
soul of mine
In your eyes, I see a world of possibilities
A future filled with love and lasting memories true
So hold my hand and lead the way
I'll follow you with all my heart, every single day
Together we'll chase our dreams and make them
With you, my love, I'll follow through.*